READING POWER

Working Together

Chefs

Joanne Mattern

The Rosen Publishing Group's
PowerKids Press™
New York

Published in 2002 by The Rosen Publishing Group, Inc.
29 East 21st Street, New York, NY 10010

Copyright © 2002 by The Rosen Publishing Group, Inc.

First Edition

Book Design: Laura Stein

Photo Credits: Maura Boruchow

Thanks to the New Orleans Cafe, Media, PA

Mattern, Joanne, 1963–
Chefs / by Joanne Mattern.
    p. cm. — (Working together (PowerKids Press))
ISBN 0-8239-5982-1 (library binding)
1. Cooks—Juvenile literature. 2. Cookery—Juvenile literature. [1.
Cooks. 2. Occupations.] I. Title. II. Series.
TX652.5 .M352 2001
641.5'023—dc21

                                                    2001000554

Manufactured in the United States of America

Contents

Meet the Chefs

We are chefs at a restaurant. We make many meals every day. Every morning we go to the market to buy fresh food.

June chooses the vegetables we will need to make our meals.

I pick out the fruit we will use today.

Getting Ready

We get ready to start our work at the restaurant. Bill and I talk about what we will cook today.

At work, we use many different tools for cooking. We hang the tools on racks.

I wear gloves when I work. The gloves keep the food clean.

June bakes bread in the oven. The bread will be ready when we open the restaurant.

Open for Business

We work as a team to make
a meal. First, a waiter enters a
customer's order into a computer.

The order is sent to the kitchen. Bill reads the order. The customer wants a salad, soup, and dessert.

I make the salad. First, I put lettuce and tomatoes on a plate. Then I put the cheese on top. Finally, I put fruit and bread on the side.

The waiter takes the salad to the customer.

June stirs the tomato soup. She uses a ladle to pour some soup into a bowl.

Ladle

17

Dessert

Together, we make an ice-cream sundae. June uses a scoop to put ice cream into a bowl. I add whipped cream and a cherry!

Scoop

19

We make food for people all day. We enjoy working together. We think that we are good cooks!

Glossary

customer (**kuhs**-tuh-muhr) a person who buys goods or services

ladle (**lay**-dl) a cup-shaped spoon with a long handle

order (**or**-duhr) a serving of food in a restaurant

racks (**raks**) frames with bars, shelves, hooks, or pegs to hold things

restaurant (**rehs**-tuh-rahnt) a place to buy and eat a meal

vegetables (**vehj**-tuh-buhlz) plants that have fruit, seeds, leaves, or roots that are used for food

waiter (**way**-tuhr) the person who brings food to customers in a restaurant

Resources

Books

Chefs
by Patricia Ryon Quiri
Compass Point Books (2000)

A Day in the Life of a Chef
by Liza N. Burby
PowerKids Press (1999)

Web Site

Cooking with Kids
http://www.weeklyreader.com/features/
   cookwka.html

Index

Word Count: 239

Note to Librarians, Teachers, and Parents

If reading is a challenge, Reading Power is a solution! Reading Power is perfect for readers who want high-interest subject matter at an accessible reading level. These fact-filled, photo-illustrated books are designed for readers who want straightforward vocabulary, engaging topics, and a manageable reading experience. With clear picture/text correspondence, leveled Reading Power books put the reader in charge. Now readers have the power to get the information they want and the skills they need in a user-friendly format.